BY THE CREATOR OF MY LITTLE ANGELS TALK TO ME

My Angels
Connections

**Short stories to
inspire and connect
YOU to your Angels**

Raúl Estévez

Copyright © 2016 by Raúl Estévez
https://www.facebook.com/raulestevezauthor/

All rights reserved. This book or any portion thereof may not be reproduced or used in any manner whatsoever without the express written permission of the author except for the use of brief quotations in a book review.

Published and distributed by
White Light Publishing House, Australia.
www.whitelightpublishing.com.au

First Printing, 2016
ISBN 978-0-9945052-1-7

Cover artwork design, layout and illustrations by Sonia Darù.

This book is not intended as a substitute for medical advice of physicians, including psychologists. The reader should regularly consult a medical professional in matters relating to his or her mental health and particularly with respect to any symptoms that may require diagnosis or medical attention. This publication contains the opinions and ideas of its author and is intended for informational purposes only.

Although the author and publisher have made every effort to ensure that the information in this book is correct, they do not assume and hereby disclaim any liability to any party for any loss, damage, or disruption caused by errors, omissions or assumptions, whether such errors or omissions result from negligence, accident, or any other cause.

White light
PUBLISHING HOUSE

**May your Angels
find their way to YOU**

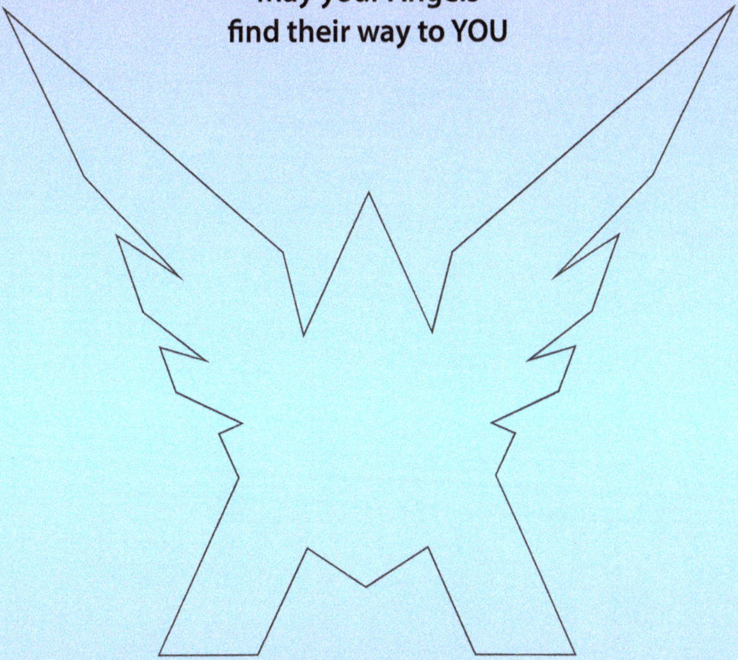

Dedication

I would like to dedicate this book to all my Angels
in heaven and on earth, you all know who you are!

Most importantly to my niece Veronica Carmona-López
for always being there for me, in the very highs
and extremely lows with unconditional love!

I love you Veronica more than words can express!

Your Tío Raúl

Acknowledgments

My sincere gratitude to my dear friends:

Sonia Darù
Sonia Darù Design
For her amazing cover artwork design, layout and illustrations,
which captured the message of this book perfectly.
You are a true artist.

Elizabeth Jane Algar, M.B.A
Director of Keilani Kava Farm, Fiji Islands
For her loving and touching foreword. You are a true
inspiration to many people, including myself.
Liz, I am proud to call you my friend!

Christie Welsh
Director of White Light Publishing House
To my publisher and editor, Christie Welsh, for her patience,
understanding and dedication to making sure my first book
delivers the message of Pure Love as I envisaged.
Very grateful to you Christie!

Contents

Introduction	15
My Story	17
Archangel Michael is my Wingman	23
Believe with all your Heart	27
Life's Graduation Day!	31
My Wish ... My Angels	35
Butterflies - Messengers from our Angels	39
A Message from Archangel Michael	43
Acknowledgment and Gratitude to the Angels	47
How I Communicate with my Angels	51
How I Met my Guardian Angel	55
A Message of Love from my Guardian Angel, Gonzalito	59
Love and Generosity	63
Shine Your Bright Light	67
Important Last Minute Message	71
Afterword	75

About the Author

Writing these true and heartfelt short stories about Angels, it has been as far removed from a thirty year career in hotel management and academia as anyone would have expected, including himself.

Raúl Estévez is a very proud Australian (born in Uruguay). His humble beginnings saw him as a houseman for an international hotel in Sydney, then he travelled the world for a few years opening five star hotels. When he returned home, Raúl found himself teaching and training for a TAFE Institute in the outer east of Melbourne, where his academic career began. Helping people learn was his passion.

Raúl returned to study and graduated from Melbourne University, with a Diploma of Teaching, followed by a Bachelor of Education and Training, and then a Master of Education. In the year 2000, whilst working for Victoria University in Melbourne, Raúl received one of the highest honours a teacher, trainer and educator could have received; 'The Vice-Chancellor's Award for Teaching Excellence'. His hospitality background coupled with his passion for helping people learn, took Raúl around the world, from Australia to Canada, Chile, Colombia, Fiji, Tonga, Vanuatu, Tuvalu, Asia, and Europe, just to name a few; training and teaching teachers and hospitality professionals alike.

Raúl's analytic and academic mind was always challenged by his belief in Angels from a very young age, but it was always close to his heart and in the back of his mind. He was blessed with having clear communication with the Angels, but in the beginning, was afraid of not being accepted by society, until a dramatic turn of events (which you will read in one of the stories) helped him see life from a different angle which allowed the Angels to then guide him more than ever.

The Angels guided Raúl to personally study with renowned authors of oracle cards and books, Doreen Virtue, Radleigh Valentine and Robert Reeves. The Angels asked him to create Crystal Blue Butterfly as a way of helping like-minded people, so they too, could receive much needed messages from their Angels. Raúl is constantly guided by them and this book was a gentle push from the Angels to share the stories with the world, because as they put it, 'Even if it helps one person it has been worthwhile sharing them'.

Foreword

Raúl Estévez has enlightened the lives of so many people around the world and will continue to do so. He is a truly gifted and accomplished Angel in education, leadership and spiritual guidance.

Whilst in the turbulence of spiralling into deep depression, Raúl was the guiding light who got me out of those dark trenches that were on the verge of swallowing me.

Raúl's crystal clear, precise and perfect timing of mentoring, Angel readings and counselling is uncanny. It touches the soul and draws deep an overwhelming realization that everything is going to be alright and it always is. Sometimes it slaps you in the face! His guidance is honest and to the point, which is grounding and healing. Raúl's wealth of knowledge is immeasurable in this field. Through his past experiences and well-travelled cultures, he feels what you are feeling and contextualizes reality in helping you to attain those things that you once thought were impossible.

For those that can face up to the truth positively, this is the best earthly guidance you will ever get. I love the sophistication and class of positive energy entwined into the readings as it keeps you yearning for more. You keep pushing your own bar to achieving excellence because Raúl's passion and kindred spirit can be felt right throughout.

I am certain that the great stories captured within this book will be felt from your very heart and soul, and will resonate with you in regards to any aspect of your life, where the valuable lessons learnt and knowledge gained can be positively shared with those you love. Enjoy the book, and may your love and light shine brightly forth.

Elizabeth Jane Algar, MBA
Director, Keilani Farm

Keilani Farm is located in the magnificent lush jungles of the high Ovalau Mountain in Fiji. Their mission is to enrich the lives of widows, single mothers and their children.

keilanikava@yahoo.com
www.facebook.com/keilanikava

Introduction

This set of thirteen* 'little' stories are about my Angels, and the connection I have and you may also have with them. The connections have been a labour of love and light, as I have been constantly guided by them, and in particular, my wingman, Archangel Michael.

They are written with love and truth in my mind and in my heart, in the hope that you the reader, can draw inspiration from them to believe in your Angels, and to open you heart and mind to listen to your own intuition, for that is one of the many ways they will communicate with us. I am not here to profess I know everything there is to know about Angels; it is a continuous learning pathway, but the one thing I know is that my communication and messages from the Angels are true and clear. As someone I trained with once told my graduating class, 'You do not need qualifications to talk to Angels; they love you for who you are. Just open your heart and listen'.

The purpose of this book is to help you open your heart and listen even more, given that you already have been listening, otherwise you would not be reading this. I wish for you to keep this book handy, so when you need some help, guidance or assistance, you may find it in one of the stories.

There are many of us out in the world willing to help you achieve your full potential by guiding you with Angels' messages. It may not be what you wish to hear, but it will always be what the Angels want you to know.

*To many people, the number thirteen carries a negative connotation, but to me, thirteen means the following:

The number thirteen means that the Ascended Masters with a female energy are with us all; reassuring us that we are moving in the right direction, and to remain positive in order to achieve our desired outcome, with faith in order to manifest all that we desire! This is the reason why I chose to include thirteen stories.

My Story

My name is Raúl.

I have been very fortunate to be able to travel around the world for more than thirty years as an international educator and trainer, offering guidance, healing and mentorship. I have had the pleasure and honour to help people learn and achieve their goals in Australia, Fiji, Malaysia, China, Singapore, Maldives, Tonga, Tuvalu, Vanuatu, Macau, Chile, Argentina, Colombia and Canada, and share my gifts, knowledge, skills and passion with some amazing people.

Early in 2014, whilst working overseas in the middle of the Indian Ocean in a beautiful place, my life was placed under threat, and I had to flee the area for my own safety and security.

This situation was a way of the Angels finally saying to me, 'Raúl, listen to us. It's time to move on and follow the next step in your Divine Life Purpose!'

As you may or may not know, Angels will often send you a feather as a message. If you do not get it, then they will throw you a brick, and if you still don't get it, they may perhaps place you in a more serious situation but still keeping you safe, for you to finally listen. Well, that is what happened to me!

Upon my return home, it was not easy at all. I had to come to terms with my life being placed under threat and it has taken years of soul searching and professional help to come to terms with having my life turned upside down.

But, 'just when the caterpillar thought the world was over, it become a butterfly,' I decided it was time to follow my spiritual and healing path and use the skills and knowledge I had attained.

On a personal level, I have had the life-long ability to speak to Angels. From a young age, I have been able to receive messages from the Angels; beginning with a relationship I had with Archangel Michael and Archangel Raphael, with whom I continue to communicate with on a daily basis.

Everything I do is guided with the best intentions. I have a passion for helping people, and I offer clear guidance from the heart, with honesty love and compassion.

Angels *Messages*

Raúl Estévez

Archangel Michael is my *Wingman*

My relationship with Archangel Michael started when I was eight years old; I was jumping over the fence from my friend's house to mine, when I collapsed and fell to the ground.

As I was laying on the ground I saw a blue light and a friendly voice said to me, 'My name is Michael. I am your Guardian Angel. I have with me my friend, Raphael and we are going to help you, just relax please!' I then saw a green emerald light surrounding me and I was placed into a healing bubble. It was a comforting feeling for me as a young boy, and I suddenly went to sleep very peacefully.

After a while, I woke up to the voice of Michael saying, 'Raúl, Raúl, wake up and look at the blue light.' I did, and then he proceeded to help me up and I was able to walk home. From that moment onwards, Archangel Michael has been my wingman; he has never left my side even in my most trying times. Even when I forgot about him or did not pay attention to him, he always gave

me a sign to let me know he was there; sometimes shocking me in order for me to listen to him.

Now, I just need to think of him and request his help and he will direct me at times to reach out and ask for help from friends and the Earth Angels community. His advice never fails me.

Lately, I have been tested; mentally, spiritually and health-wise, however, Archangel Michael is there to guide me to the right person who will help me realise how fortunate I am to live in a country that looks after me well. I am very fortunate to have him in my daily life!

Angels
Messages

Use this space to record any of your own messages from your angels that you receive via your dreams, thoughts, feelings and intuition.

Believe with *all your Heart*

A message from our Angels

It's never fun going through medical issues and treatments, however, as I am dealing with them and embracing treatments, the wait-lists to see a surgeon/specialist, the ups and downs of my physical being, my mind and my EGO, the Angels are always by my side; taking care of me, guiding me and telling me, 'Raúl, you are where you are meant to be in order to learn certain lessons and to continue to help others.'

Although at times, these lessons can be very painful in many ways, I know they are necessary for my growth and EVOLution (as many of you may have experienced yourself).

The ultimate message is to 'Believe with all your heart.'

Things will always improve, the sun shines after the rain, and it's important to remember that both are necessary for everything to grow and flourish!

Look for the rainbow of HOPE!

Archangel Raphael tells me, 'Raúl, you are loved and I am guiding you to your healers in all forms and modalities. You are doing great! Just think of me, and I shall be by your side ready to help you heal, just ask!'

We must open up our hearts, listen to our messages though our thoughts and intuition, and allow ourselves to be guided. You deserve to love and to be loved!

When I do a reading or healing session for a client I request of them that they 'Believe with all their heart!'

When using Quantum Bioenergetics, healing always takes place. It may not be exactly the area you expect to heal, because the quantum frequencies react to your body's priority of what needs to heal first, but healing does occur at a cellular level.

When doing an Angel card reading, it might not be exactly what you want to hear, but it is always what the Angels would like you to know in order for you to take action and grow!

My Angels Connections

I would like to thank Archangel Raphael and Archangel Michael, for clearly guiding me, encouraging me and supporting me in my healing work, and for guiding the right clients to me, so that I may be of service and help them always.

Forever grateful! I believe with all my heart!

Love and light always,
Raúl, your Angelic Messenger

Remember...
Believe in Angels, because they do believe in you!

Life's Graduation Day

A message from Archangel Michael

In one of my conversations with Archangel Michael I asked him, 'What happens when we die?'

His response was, 'Raúl, life is like a school or university. You go through life attending different classes, continuously learning – you sit for tests and exams – many times you pass with flying colours, other times you don't; however, learning still takes place, then you reach the end of the course, and the most awaited day that you have been looking forward to, has arrived: Graduation Day!'

'On that day people will be with you, or in touch with you from near and far to celebrate your achievements! So, you see Raúl, death is your graduation day; you have reached the end of your course in this life time and now you are ready to graduate. Your soul will carry the knowledge of all lessons learnt across the Bridge of Light, guided and still protected by me with my sword of truth and my blue light. When the time is right, it will happen

to you and everyone in different ways, then…at the other end of the bridge, loved ones who have passed away before you will be there to celebrate with you on your Life's Graduation Day!'

'Now you will be able to see each other's souls and become LOVE! Remember Raúl, during the course of your life, to fly high on the wings of Gratitude!'

Thank you, Archangel Michael, for guiding and protecting us always!

Love and light always,
Raúl, your Angelic Messenger

Remember…
Believe in Angels, because they do believe in you!

My Angels Connections

Angels
Messages

Use this space to record any of your own messages from your angels that you receive via your dreams, thoughts, feelings and intuition.

Raúl Estévez

My Wish ...
My Angels

We all know the old saying 'When you wish upon a star...' My Angels have always told me to believe with all my heart and my dreams will come true. Indeed, they have. Ever since I was a teenager, I wanted to be a 'citizen of the world.' Little did I know, that my middle sister Cristina would sponsor my parents and I to live in Australia; what a blessing this action of love and kindness was!

Although it was not simple, and there were many hurdles to overcome, my Angels were always there offering encouragement and giving me/us a never-give-up attitude which has stuck with me forever. I have been so blessed to have forged a great career here at home in Australia that has allowed me to be of service to people around the world. I have been to places that some people only dream of. Thank you, Angels!

Even in my darkest hour when I thought I had lost everything (material things, that is), the Angels showed me that in fact, I had found everything! I had found my true self! 'Less is more' became the new 'normal'; if I can't afford it, I don't need it. I started focusing on what I have and being truly grateful instead of focussing on what I have not. This was the hardest, but most rewarding lesson of all.

Abundance does not always mean money; it means health, or being able to accept a helping hand from a family member or friend when I needed it most. A few examples of abundance:

- I won tickets to a show when I wanted to go, and the cash was not there.
- My niece Veronica and her husband Daniel who have six children, reorganised their lives in Sydney so Veronica could be with me at several times of need.
- My nephew Dario and his wife Tanya purchasing airline tickets as a gift to me so I could fly and be with family for Christmas 2015.
- My dear friend Catherine offering me emotional and a couple of times, financial support (which I managed to repay).
- My sister Marilyn and my niece Sandra in Orlando USA. Marilyn always helping me with Reiki and returning the favour with my Angels and both of them recommending me to friends, all of them blessings from our Angels.
- Nieces and nephew surprising me with flowers and a little present when it was least expected.

My Angels Connections

So, the common denominator here is abundance in love! I find myself at times, helping to brighten up the day of another person with a smile, or a punnet of strawberries, even if it's someone I will never meet or never get a thank you from; that is abundance!

My wingman, Archangel Michael, has been guiding me to just trust, let go and allow. I don't need to be in control all the time; that is in the past.

From now on, I wish for the best possible outcome and I allow my Angels to work behind the scenes with the Creator to bring my wishes to me in divine timing. I always listen to their guidance and take the necessary action to make those dreams and wishes manifest into my reality. The difference is, I am no longer forcing things to happen; I am simply allowing!

My heart is opening more and more every day, and the more I help people receive messages from their Angels, the more I realise how accurate my Angels were when they told me to be of help and service to others through my gifts.

Thank you, Archangel Michael. I am in awe of your faith in me and your continuous guidance. Thank you for showing me that everything I have experienced and been through had a great purpose: to help me realise my Divine Life Purpose.

Love and light always,
Raúl, your Angelic Messenger

Remember...
Believe in Angels, because they do believe in you!

Butterflies
Messengers from our Angels

My late mother, one of my Angels in heaven before she passed away told me, 'Raúl every time you see a butterfly it will bring a beautiful message from me to you!' How true this became; on my university graduation day whilst proudly taking pictures a beautiful white butterfly flew by and circled me! Tears of love and joy rolled down my face. Wow, thanks Mum!

I have been very fortunate that my job has taken me many times around the world helping people learn (and also learning myself) and being of service to people, and without fail in every country/every city, even when snowing, Mum sent me a butterfly to greet me and to let me know I was on the right path of my Divine Life Purpose. I've always felt so blessed!

Today as I mature and go through the struggles of life and learning lessons as a loving and magnificent soul living a human experience, the butterflies and messages keep on coming. Every day I see butterflies; they show up on a picture or on someone's tshirt, however, Mum's message is always there, beautiful and clear. I am loved, I give love to others and I love myself too! The butterflies carry that voice of encouragement that tells me, 'Please keep going, the best is yet to come!'

Today, as I sat here, recovering and healing in the garden under the shade of a beautiful pine tree, listening to the water from the fountain trickling, surrounded by Mother Nature and my Angels, feeling grateful, a gorgeous little white butterfly flew by in front of me. I looked up and said, 'Thank you.' The gorgeous butterfly rested upon a flower and gave me the chance of taking a photo (which is the one headlining this story). By the way, my late mother's name was Blanca which means 'white' in Spanish. So, thank you for the message Mum, I believe with all my heart!

We go through this lifetime learning, helping, transforming, evolving and emerging as beautiful butterflies. So, from now on, every time YOU see a butterfly, know that an Angel in heaven is sending you a positive and encouraging message: 'Believe in yourself.'

In order to help and be of service to others, we must allow ourselves to emerge gloriously from the chrysalis as a beautiful butterfly, and fly to their assistance. 'Believe with all your heart.' Thank you Mum and Archangel Michael for guiding and protecting me always!

Love and light always,
Raúl, your Angelic Messenger

Post scriptum: The very day this book was launched, which was outdoors, a white butterfly flew between the audience and I. As I was delivering my speech, people in the audience said 'did you see it Raúl?' Which I replied 'yes', looked up to the sky and said 'thank you Mum!'

Remember...
Believe in Angels, because they do believe in you!

Raúl Estévez

A Message from
Archangel Michael

One day whilst trying not to think about all my medical issues and sitting outside in the backyard amongst the trees, plants and flowers, enjoying what Mother Nature has to offer, the following message came through:

Dear Raúl,

This is Archangel Michael, talking to you and letting you know that everything that you have done in your life has led you to this moment, where you are ready to receive my message loud and clear with positive intention and conviction.

You are loved; you have always been, and always will be a unique soul created in likeness and perfection of the Creator of all that is! Keep on sending your love to everyone, everywhere. You are ready for your divine life mission.

Crystal Blue Butterfly is only your starting point; there is so much more on it is way to you. Simply be patient, follow advice

and guidance, and allow myself and all the Angels to help you. I am guiding you to people, situations and teachers who will be there to assist you. Please don't be afraid; jump in with all your heart and passion, because what you have to offer everyone, it is real, it is pure positive intent, it is LOVE! Myself and the other Archangels and Angels are here as your support team; guiding you every step of the way.

You are coming out of the darkness into the light just like a caterpillar inside a cocoon, transforming into a butterfly and breaking free from it. You are ready to fly and show your beautiful colours to the world. Success is yours for the taking; you know it, and so do we.

Raúl, you have done everything right by allowing yourself to go through the dark times and places in order to shine your pure light on everything, everywhere and everyone. We, the Angels love you, and know how hard you have worked all your life.

YOU ARE READY, please enjoy!

Much love,

Archangel Michael and the League of Angels

Remember...
Believe in Angels, because they do believe in you!

My Angels Connections

Angels
Messages

Use this space to record any of your own messages from your Angels that you receive via your dreams, thoughts, feelings and intuition.

Raúl Estévez

Acknowledgment and Gratitude
to the Angels

Lately, I have been guided by my Angels to write, and to share the messages I receive, and to trust.

Something I have known for many years is to listen to my intuition because that is where my Angels deliver their messages clearly in my own voice. Knowing that they are guiding me on my Divine Life Purpose to not only help others, but through my writing, also helps me.

I aim to help people heal with my abilities and skills, but most importantly, with my short stories, to show them that they are not alone, and what they hear in their minds is truly clear guidance from their Angels, so long as they listen with an open and positive heart minus their negative ego. By going deep inside my soul and tapping into the healing realm that exists within me to help others heal with the Angels and to achieve the results in my life that I so desire; transformation through belief and healing.

Thank you Angels from my heart and soul for sending me this message to not give up and not give in with my writing, and to share it. I keep my trust and faith with an open heart that my messages and stories will touch the hearts of those who need it, and so it is!

Remember...
Believe in Angels, because they do believe in you!

My Angels Connections

Angels
Messages

Use this space to record any of your own messages from your Angels that you receive via your dreams, thoughts, feelings and intuition.

How I Communicate
with my Angels

Nowadays, I just think of a particular Angel such as Archangel Michael, and ask for his help, and he delivers every time for me. It is always what I need for my highest good.

However, the most effective way for us to talk is during quiet time/meditation. Please do not be 'put off' by the word meditation. To me, it means sitting in my favourite comfy chair, with very soft relaxing music in the background and just allowing my thoughts and intuition to flow freely without forcing them.

You could do this whilst having a relaxing bath, surrounded with beautiful scented candles, allowing the water to take your worries away and carry them to the Creator to assist you, or it could be a three-minute shower meditation (we need to be water conscious and preserve that important resource). Simply allow the water from the shower to hit the top of your head or Crown Chakra, and envision this water flowing though all your energetic centers; cleansing and removing all unwanted

energies, and disposing of them through the bottom of your feet into the drain; to be transmuted by the Angels and Creator into light.

You may also decide to take a relaxing walk along the foreshore at the beach, allowing the beauty of the salt water to cleanse your mind, body and soul, or if the temperature permits, swim in it!

I sometimes go to my local botanical garden and enjoy the beauty of the trees, plants and flowers. After all, Mother Nature smiles to us through flowers.

Stop at a white rose bush and take its scent; allowing Archangel Raphael to help purify you with its energy.

Place a blanket under a tree and observe its trunk, branches, and leaves, and absorb its healing, love and precious oxygen they provide us. Give thanks for the wonders of the Creator!

Perhaps as I do, you may find solace in writing your thoughts in a journal. Whether it's paper based or electronic, simply allow the messages to flow freely without placing any sort of judgment about what you are writing about.

Meditation could take many forms, so long as you find time daily to connect with your inner self, inner child or your soul.

Love and light always,
Raúl, your Angelic Messenger

Remember...
Believe in Angels, because they do believe in you!

Raúl Estévez

How I Met my
Guardian Angel

Although I always knew I had a Guardian Angel, I did not get to meet him until May 2016. Angels surround us all, and Archangels in particular can be of help simultaneously to everyone, however a Guardian Angel is assigned to each one of us and we don't share them. During a healing session with a beautiful and generous Earth Angel from Queensland in Australia named Jeanette, my Guardian Angel was revealed to me.

I have always had a very close link to Machu Pichu in Peru (I have not yet been there). A ten year old boy with dark hair, olive skin and a cheeky smile wearing a white tunic with a golden rope-like belt around his waist, introduced himself to me by the name of Gonzalito. There he was, standing with the background of Machu Pichu in all its glory (not as we see it today). You could say that rather than wings, he has a beautiful golden energy around him. At one point I pronounced his name as 'Gonzalo', and with his cheeky personality, he let me know he is Gonzalito, reminding me that while he may only be ten years old, he is a

very wise old soul, so I obliged, and Gonzalito it is! We continued to have a conversation, and I said, 'I would like to express my greatest gratitude to you for showing yourself in my life right now,' to which he replied, 'I have always been with you, but it's only now you are ready to see me and talk to me, because you have found the Holy Trinity within you; mind, body and soul coming into alignment.'

Gonzalito, I will endeavour to follow your guidance and for you to continue showing me your amazing golden light and aura. I am now ready to receive the abundance you are sending me on every level of my life, including my spiritual, physical and financial well-being. I am so grateful for everything and everyone in my life right now, and I sense a beautiful feeling of anticipation for the amazing gifts you will be sharing with me. Please continue talking to me, and showing me the way with your golden light to fulfil my beautiful and Divine Life Purpose.

I love you Gonzalito, and thank you!

Love and light always,
Raúl, your Angelic Messenger

Remember...
Believe in Angels, because they do believe in you!

My Angels Connections

Angels
Messages

Use this space to record any of your own messages from your Angels that you receive via your dreams, thoughts, feelings and intuition.

A message of *Love*

from my Guardian Angel, Gonzalito

Dear Raúl,

*The way forward is the only way you already know; 'LOVE.'
Keep loving your life and everything in it.*

Do not fight disease; simply send it love.

Who you are today is exactly who you are meant to become.

Do not judge yourself. You are our Angelic Messenger.

There are lots of people coming your way, beautiful soul living a human experience with an opened heart, and there will be a beautiful exchange of energy for your beautiful services as an Angelic Messenger and Psychic Healer. Because you give your gifts with great honesty and love, and they feel your great help and assistance to fulfil their own Divine Life Purpose, they will recommend you to so many more beautiful souls living a human experience. Keep walking along your pathway of love.

I, your Guardian Angel Gonzalito, am here shining my golden light along your divine pathway, so please do not fear bumps along the road, as I will guide you to overcome them.

Raúl, believe and trust that great abundance is coming to you in every way possible to help you and others. Jeannette is right; June 2016 is going to be a month of significant abundance, flowing with great benefits to you and others who receive your gifts. You will start receiving all the help in material and non-material ways that you so deserve and desire for your life to continue to flourish, and in turn, helping others to flourish.

*Move towards the golden light
I am showing you with faith and love!*

Your Guardian Angel Gonzalito

Remember...
Believe in Angels, because they do believe in you!

My Angels Connections

Angels
Messages

**Use this space to record any of your own messages
from your Angels that you receive via your dreams,
thoughts, feelings and intuition.**

Raúl Estévez

Love and *Generosity*

As I sit here guided by my Angels, including my Guardian Angel Gonzalito, a beautiful feeling of unconditional love and generosity comes over me and engulfs me in a gorgeous golden orb, providing me with the sanctuary I need at this time. I feel guided and compelled to write about being generous and unconditional love. I've sent this feeling out to everyone, and I encourage you do the same as you read this (even to those who have done you wrong).

My heart is fully opened to send and receive love. It will push us forward to a clear understanding of who we are. We are one. This oneness still allows us to be the perfect and unique soul, living a human experience that we can be!

I love where I am now (all the great stuff and the not so great). It has taken me many lifetimes to get here, many lessons were learnt; some harsh ones, and many, many beautiful ones. I have learnt to love myself and be generous to myself in order to do the

same for others; something that I did not do before. My Angels tell me that in this, my ascension journey, I will continue to learn more and more. I feel the joy in my heart, and in turn I am sending this joy to everyone and everything around the world, around the universe and beyond.

Remember that with people, even if they are wrong in their belief and values (from your point of view), they are right because that is what they believe in. You cannot change others if they do not want to change, but you can change your reaction to their thoughts and feelings.

Please understand, I am not saying you need to be a doormat and accept their views; I am simply saying release the feelings and let these people go if they are no longer part of your story. People come into our lives for a reason; a season or a lifetime, keep this in mind. Let them go with pure love, for when we send pure love into the world for others, the universe will return that love to us one thousand fold. Today, I am living my life from a place of happiness, love and gratitude (regardless of the issues or problems I have to face). When I face them from a place of love, all is well. I am sending this love to you, the reader.

As I write these words, beautiful Angels, including my Ascended Master, and Gonzalito, my Guardian Angel, surround me. They are all raising Gonzalito up with their energy in the form of wings so I can see him (he is only a ten year old boy, remember). He says to me, 'Raúl, you are finally taking care of you, the Holy Trinity; mind, body and soul, including your inner child, who once again smiles with love, compassion, understanding and gratitude.' And, so it is! Thank you!

Love and light always,
Raúl, your Angelic Messenger

Remember...
Believe in Angels, because they do believe in you!

Raúl Estévez

Shine Your *Bright Light!*

My Angels compel me once again and the Ascended Masters, who are right here with me and with you, stand before me, behind me and all around me, to deliver this message for you today.

The first thing they would like say to us is, 'Don't define yourself by somebody else's standards, but your own.'

'They are saying that you, and you alone can conquer your own ego and allow your divine true self to emerge, by allowing your soul and inner light to shine as bright as possible.'

'The time has come for you, Earth Angels, to join in, and I call upon you all to dig deep inside and take a deep breath, place both hands on your heart chakra and open your hands, and share your love and light with everyone. Imagine your light shining above you; your own space, the room, your suburb, your city, your state, your country, go above the earth, right above the

universe and shine your love! You owe it to yourself and to us all, to be the perfect unique you! Dear Earth Angels, it is time for us all to spread our wings and live our Divine Life Purpose!'

Now, my Guardian would like to talk about the words we use. First they like to talk about a word used by many: 'FAIL.' Gonzalito is asking you to remove the fear from that word, and only to think of it as 'first attempt in learning.'

We forget at times, that we are souls living a human experience, so let us allow ourselves to learn and move forward; not holding on to fear or pain, but to hold on to the lessons we have learnt in our 'first attempt in learning.'

Other words we use as well are, 'I am battling or fighting a certain illness or disease.' Please don't declare war on your situation; instead choose to be happy, knowing that by sending love to your current situation or dis-ease (not being at ease), that love and only love will be returned to you. Suddenly, the Angels will guide you to the best medical care available.

Almost a year ago, I needed to have an operation, and doctors and specialists kept telling me I would be on a one year waitlist. Well, I asked the Angels with all my love to deliver a message to the Creator to guide me to the best possible outcome available,

and I put a note on my Angel box*. I was then guided to a new specialist who contacted a hospital in Melbourne, and within a month and a half, the operation took place. I did not fight or battle it; I've simply sent love and allowed the Angels to help me. I still have other health issues that need resolving, but I do not push; I allow the best to come to me and slowly but surely, it does.

*An Angel box is simple to create. I bought a lovely box, placed a picture of an Angel that resonated with me, and inside I put a note to the Angels to give them permission to act on my behalf, because Angels respect our free will, and will not act without our permission.

My Angels love me, and your Angels love you, too. Keep the faith, and HOPE: Have Only Positive Expectations.

Angel Blessings,

Raúl, your Angelic Messenger

Remember...
Believe in Angels, because they do believe in you!

Raúl Estévez

Important
Last Minute Message

Archangel Metatron is the Angel who helps us deepen our connection with the Creator. This Archangel just came to me and kindly asked me to include this little message in the book, so how can I deny such a beautiful request?

He/she (as I believe Angels to be beings of energy and light who carry both masculine and feminine energies which will resonate with us in different ways) just came to me to tell me/us all, that the path of a Lightworker is not always an easy or simple one, but our attitude of love determines how we feel and react to overcome the challenges presented to us.

Archangel Metatron walks alongside us, to show us that our strength – or more importantly – our inner strength is our true leader, because this is where we find the strength of our Creator.

Archangel Metatron is urging us to touch people's heart, by leading from the heart. We must walk our own pathway of strength and Archangel Metatron highlights that many people in our human history have been judged harshly by others for being a strong Lightworker. These Lightworkers shone their own light in order to inspire others to shine their own inner lights, without the fear or threat of competition, but simply like a flower blooming to give us love!

Metatron is offering me and us, all the beautiful Flowers of Life from the Tree of Life (whom he is the Guardian of) and it's very clear and bright in its sacred geometry (also known as Metatron's cube).

This is provided to us in order to motivate us, heal us and encourage us in our diving pathway. He/she is also here to help us clear any lower energies with hope and love; moving forward in our ascension as a soul enjoying our human experience.

Archangel Metatron tells me that when we feel low, moody or irritable, to call upon him and he will come to our aid; removing all blocks and to remind us that Archangels can help us all simultaneously. So, it's important to know that we don't bother them by our heartfelt requests; they cherish our request for help.

I close this last minute message with a prayer:

Dear Archangel Metatron,

Please remove all lower energies that no longer serve us and guide us all to continue to develop our spiritual gifts so we can be of service to all with pure love in our hearts.

Knowing that our intentions are only to love and being loved, for we are one.

Thank you!

And so it is.

Afterword

Dear Earth Angels,

Times are changing and we as individuals are re-awakening to a new/old world and reality. We are one, we are all connected, and we are beings of energy just like our Angels, however, with a physical body living a human experience. Be inspired to become the best you can, and desire to be, but do not be too hard on yourself. Be a human; allow yourself that permission. We Angels live in that fourth dimension that you as humans cannot yet perceive or comprehend; we are just beyond the veil, simply believe with all your heart.

We the Angels, know that at your core – at your soul level – you know us, because we have welcomed you back into a human experience many times before. Please know that Angels do exist; perhaps not so much in the form we show you through your human eyes and perception, but as beings of pure light, love and energy.

And so it is.

Other titles by Raúl Estévez

My Little Angels Talk To Me
Author: Raúl Estévez
Illustrator: Sonia Darù

A delightful children's book created with the intention of sparking the imagination and curiosity within every child, and to promote playing outside with fun and love! It also includes detachable colouring in pages at the back of the book.

Guiding Star of Life Inspirational Cards
Author: Raúl Estévez
Illustrator: Sonia Darù

Based on his daily Angel Card readings, Raúl's 44 card deck, guidance card and guidebook allows you to find inspiration using a uniquely designed four-point Guiding Star of Life.

Upcoming Title

Why Do Doggies Sniff Their Tails When They Meet?

Author: Raúl Estévez
Illustrator: Sonia Darù

*'Tell me Grandma, why do doggies sniff their tails
every time they meet?'*

*'Well Raúlito,' answered Grandma Morocha,
'let me tell you a story!'*

*Raúl recalls the wonder instilled in him by the story telling
of his beautiful Grandma Morocha of indeed why anywhere
Raúl saw dogs they would be sniffing their tails!*

*Join the little doggies in Doggyville as they excitedly
prepare for the inaugural Doggy Masquerade Ball ...
where they leave more than their coats at the door!*

For more information regarding Raúl and the services he offers please visit:
https://www.facebook.com/raulestevezauthor/

What goes around comes around,
so I decided to send Love

EVOL*ution*
through Love!

A final word from the

Author

May all of your dreams and
desires come true - but one -
so you will always have
something wonderful
to look forward to,
work toward
and manifest.

Raúl
Your Angelic Messenger

www.ingramcontent.com/pod-product-compliance
Lightning Source LLC
Chambersburg PA
CBHW040330300426
44113CB00020B/2712